Original title:
Taking My Magic Back

Copyright © 2024 Book Fairy Publishing
All rights reserved.

Editor: Theodor Taimla
Author: Claudia Kuma
ISBN HARDBACK: 978-9916-759-20-2
ISBN PAPERBACK: 978-9916-759-21-9

Glimmers of Forgotten Spells

In shadows deep, where whispers dwell,
Glimmers of forgotten spells,
Ancient runes on parchment frail,
Stories lost, yet to unveil.

Stars align with secret light,
Mysteries dancing in the night,
Hands reach out with guarded care,
Magic sifts through twilight's air.

Enchanted woods where echoes play,
Wisps of spells in disarray,
Fingers trace the hidden lore,
Ancient paths to realms explore.

Silent halls, where time forgot,
Echoes of a spellbound plot,
Mystic symbols fade and gleam,
Glimmers of a sorcerer's dream.

Within the night, the secrets call,
Forgotten spells, they rise and fall,
Through the ages, whispers tell,
Of glimmers from that ancient spell.

The Phoenix Conjuration

From ashes, whispers start anew,
Phoenix flames in crimson hue,
Wings of fire, rise so high,
In a blaze, it claims the sky.

Selves reborn in sacred light,
A spell weaves through the darkest night,
Myth and magic, intertwined,
In fervent flames, a life refined.

Burst of life from ember's core,
Mystics chant and spirits soar,
Circle round the phoenix bright,
Guardians of eternal light.

In the flames, old tales ignite,
Truths unfold by fiery sight,
Legends breath through burning air,
Phoenix conjured with great care.

Rebirth echoes through the land,
Ancient rites by fire's command,
Phoenix calls, and lives restore,
Magic lives forevermore.

Reviving the Sorcerer's Flame

In the depths where shadows reign,
Lies the sorcerer's hidden flame,
Guardians of the ancient spark,
Echoes haunt the endless dark.

Candles flicker, secrets hide,
Magic stirs from deep inside,
Rituals in moonlight's glow,
Revive the flame where mystics go.

Hands trace old, enchanted signs,
Words recall forgotten lines,
Fires flare with mystic blaze,
Sorcerer's flame in twilight's haze.

Charms invoke the arcane lore,
Fueled by spells from days of yore,
Wisps of power in shadows claim,
Reviving the sorcerer's flame.

Through the veils where secrets blend,
Mystic fires rise again,
In the hush, the whispers call,
To the flame, surrender all.

Restoring Enchanted Voices

Whispers weave through twilight's veil,
Enchantments lost in stories pale,
Voices call from realms unseen,
Restoring magic's silken sheen.

In old woods where silence clings,
Echoes flutter on phantom wings,
Chants arise from hidden places,
Ancient songs in secret spaces.

Moonlit lakes reflect the past,
Voices rise and spells are cast,
Ripples hold the ancient rhymes,
Echoes of forgotten times.

Mystic chords from shadows deep,
Sung by spirits as they keep,
Memories of enchanted songs,
Restoring where the heart belongs.

Through the night, the voices mend,
Magic whispers without end,
In soft murmurs, truth rejoices,
Restoring all enchanted voices.

Sorcery Reinstated

The winds of magic blow anew,
Across the plains so green,
With whispers old and powers true,
In realms once left unseen.

The ancient rites, they shimmer bright,
In twilight's mystic glow,
A dance of shadows, dark and light,
Where hidden secrets flow.

The elders chant in tongues unknown,
Their voices rise and fall,
Reviving spells in twilight's tone,
Enchantment's ancient call.

Crystals gleam in moonlit haze,
Runes ignite the night,
Mysteries of forgotten days,
Now brought to brilliant light.

In covens deep, the sorcerers meet,
Their powers reinstated,
With whispered vows in circles steep,
Their destinies are fated.

Arcane Comeback

From dusty tomes and sacred scrolls,
The echoes of the past,
Arcane arts reclaim their roles,
In spells now cast.

The sigils carved in ancient stone,
By hands of times gone by,
Awaken powers, once unknown,
Beneath the starlit sky.

Wizards weave with fingers deft,
The magic of old lore,
Resurrecting spells they left,
To wander evermore.

Candles flicker, shadows dance,
In the circle of rebirth,
Where mystic forces take a chance,
To find their place on earth.

Old incantations, softly spoken,
In whispered mystery,
The ancient seals, once now broken,
The arcane set free.

Fabled Powers Revived

Time-worn lore of fabled might,
In crypts long sealed away,
Revived beneath the silver light,
Of a moonlit, arcane day.

The heroes' tales, their legends strong,
Awaken from their sleep,
With chants that echo ancient song,
Their promises to keep.

An aurora of enchanted hue,
Illuminates the night,
Where fabled powers, once they grew,
Return to mortal sight.

Magicians old, their secrets guard,
In chambers dark and deep,
With wisdom from the stars unmarred,
The powers, they upkeep.

In whispers soft, the magic flows,
Reviving all that's prized,
The timeless strength, the world now knows,
Fabled powers revived.

Enchantment Rewoven

A tapestry of magic spun,
With threads both old and new,
In twilight's glow, an ancient run,
Enchantment now renew.

The weavers of the mystic arts,
With hands so deft and light,
Rebind the spells in sacred charts,
And bring them into sight.

Glistening stars in velvet sky,
Guide the woven threads,
Binding light and dark to tie,
In spells the heart now dreads.

With every knot, a secret told,
In murmurs soft and low,
The tales of ages, dark and bold,
Within the fabric flow.

Enchantment's weave, now redefined,
In patterns rich and grand,
Rewoven magic, intertwined,
To grace the mortal land.

The Awakening of Arcane Light

In twilight's breath, the whispers rise,
Arcane light in shadowed skies.
Mystic glow awakens night,
Darkness yields to dawning sight.

Ethereal realms in ancient lore,
Guarded secrets from days of yore.
Wisps of magic, softly flare,
Illuminating the silent air.

From the depths of time's embrace,
Enigmas dance, leave no trace.
Symbols drawn in silver hue,
Binding realms of old to new.

As moonlight weaves its spectral thread,
Dreams entwine in cosmic dread.
Awakening the light's refrain,
Mystic powers come to reign.

Veil lifted, worlds unite,
In the heart of arcane light.
Chants resound, the spells complete,
In the dawn, their spirits meet.

Summoning the Lost Magicka

In the crypts of ancient days,
Silent echoes, mystic haze.
Lost magicka, once revered,
Calls beneath, forever feared.

Stars align in cosmic dance,
Casting light on fate's expanse.
Whispers from the void emerge,
Energies begin to surge.

Runes inscribed in hidden tome,
Summon forth forgotten home.
Elemental spirits rise,
Hidden truths within their eyes.

Rituals of time untold,
Mystic forces fierce and bold.
Lost magicka, reclaim thy might,
From the depths, return to light.

Woven spells ignite the night,
Ancient powers take their flight.
Boundless realms, a sacred key,
Summoning eternity.

Resurgence of the Mystic Heart

In the quiet of the soul,
Mystic heart begins to roll.
Echoes of a whispered chant,
Emanate from distant plant.

Deep within the forest air,
Magic weaves without compare.
Resurgence of the heart so bright,
Guided by celestial light.

From the ashes, hope is born,
In the glow of mystic morn.
Renewed strength within the beat,
Ancient rhythms, wild and sweet.

Cosmic forces interlace,
Binding time and sacred space.
Resurgence of the heart's decree,
Unlocking universal key.

Harmony in every strand,
Mystic heart takes its stand.
In the now, eternity,
Resurges with pure clarity.

Casting the Circle Anew

Underneath the starlit dome,
Circle formed like ancient home.
Casting spells with whispered lore,
Mysteries rekindled, more.

Elements in balance bind,
Magic's essence, intertwined.
Sacred rites in moonlight's hue,
Casting the circle anew.

Candles lit, intentions set,
Shadows dance, the stage is met.
Energy flows in harmonic stream,
Envisioned through a waking dream.

Guardians of the spirits' gate,
Witness eons, seal the fate.
In the circle's shimmering blaze,
New beginnings now will raise.

Bound by love and spirit's quest,
Ancient powers manifest.
Casting wide the circle's light,
In unity, we take our flight.

Reclaiming Mystical Power

In shadows deep where secrets lie,
Lost arcs of magic, wisp and fly.
Beyond the veils of mundane sight,
Awakens power in the night.

Symbols etched on ancient bark,
Spoken words ignite the spark.
Hands of old guide through the lore,
Unlocking realms, creating door.

Mystic winds and whispers hear,
Echoes of the hinter sphere.
In the circle, timeless, found,
Power reclaimed, unbound, unbound.

The Phoenix's Spells Recalled

From ashes cold, a spark revives,
A tale of magic, bound by lives.
Phoenix rise, your fire dance,
Spellbound worlds in mystic trance.

Feathers weave the twilight's code,
Flickering, the embers showed.
Ancient words in flames compile,
Casting spells through endless miles.

In rebirth's light, a spell defined,
Binding hearts, transcending time.
Phoenix's call, the ancient thrall,
Summons magic, one and all.

Wandering in Mystical Realms

Through misty paths and shadowed trees,
A wanderer drifts with gentle breeze.
Beyond the world of toil and steel,
To realms where deeper truths reveal.

Whispering winds, the secrets share,
Mystic lands with beauty rare.
Each step a journey towards the core,
Of magic's touch and ancient lore.

Stars align in patterns old,
Guiding souls, the mystery unfolds.
In silence, realms of wonder brought,
Wandering, mystic realms are sought.

Resurrecting Hidden Charms

In forgotten nooks, where shadows play,
Hidden charms in twilight stay.
Long-lost spells of worlds bygone,
Whispered on the dawn's first yawn.

With penchant for the hidden art,
Revive the charm from ancient start.
Silent incantations hum,
Awakening secrets, faintly sung.

From olden pages, dust removed,
Resurrecting, magic proved.
Hidden charms in hands now hold,
Timeless power, new and bold.

The Charms Restored

In ancient books, bound tight with lore,
Lies magic lost in days of yore.
With whispered words and binding spell,
Its power we shall once more tell.

Through forests dark and rivers wide,
The seekers of the secrets stride.
For every charm unfairly shunned,
A tale of wonder now begun.

The moonlight casts a silver thread,
To guide the steps where ancients tread.
With hands entwined, they call anew,
The magic skies, a mystic hue.

The charms restored, a fervent flame,
Revives the olden, hallowed name.
The silence breaks with echoes grand,
A symphony of Arcane's hand.

In hearts once barren, life renews,
Through spells that ancient paths infuse.
The world transformed, the ancient lores,
Speak softly now through open doors.

Reviving the Forgotten Art

In shadows deep where echoes sleep,
Lies hidden craft, a past to reap.
The hands of time now carve and trace,
Forgotten art in silent space.

Beneath the dust of years unborn,
The whispers of the old adorn.
From tenebrous, the spark ignites,
Reviving art through endless nights.

Each brush a tale of yester's dream,
Each stroke restores the ancient theme.
In every hue, a history,
Unveiled in vivid mystery.

The whispers grow, the shadows fade,
An artist's spirit, unafraid.
With every touch, forgotten dreams,
Revive in colors, vivid schemes.

The past's embrace now softly yields,
A canvas wide, enchanted fields.
Reviving art with hands and heart,
A timeless dance, a sacred part.

From Ashes to Incantations

From ashes cold, where embers fade,
The mystic chants once more invade.
The silent air with whispers bright,
Transforms the night with ancient light.

In rituals, the essence sown,
To realms unknown, the spirits flown.
Through circles cast and sigils wired,
The magic born from flames admired.

The ancient tongues in harmony,
Invoke the soul's deep alchemy.
From cinders rise the potent spells,
Through resonant and sacred wells.

The ashes gray, their memories keep,
Awakened now from silent sleep.
Incantations deeply spun,
Revive the age of spells begun.

From phoenix burn a life reclaimed,
The arcane fires unbound, untamed.
In sacred rites, the whispers sing,
From ashes rise, the magic's spring.

The Twilight Magic Returns

At twilight's edge, in dusk's embrace,
The magic stirs with secret grace.
A symphony of shadows blend,
Where night and day in silence mend.

The twilight calls with whispered hues,
Its mystery in softest blues.
With starlit skies and moon's soft gleam,
The twilight world becomes a dream.

The ancient spirits start to dance,
In twilight's spell, a trance's chance.
With every breath, the night secures,
The hidden lore of ages' cures.

In twilight's veil, the mystics spin,
The threads of time, they weave within.
Old magic wakes in darkened light,
Returning in the dim twilight.

The magic flows in twilight's reign,
A whispering, enchanting chain.
In twilight's arms, the night restores,
The magic world it ever stores.

The Enchanter's Renaissance

In twilight's veiled embrace,
The enchanter sings her spell,
Whispers dance on misty lace,
Where olden secrets dwell.

Lanterns lit by ancient flame,
Guiding lost souls home,
Magic circles, pagan names,
Across the starry dome.

Runes carved with weathered hands,
Spellbound wands take flight,
Reviving dreams from distant lands,
In the still of night.

Chants that pierce the dawn,
Mystery's soft refrain,
Echoes of a world reborn,
Evermore sustain.

In shadows deep, a yarn etwines,
Of realms unseen, immense,
The enchanter's craft defines,
A timeless renaissance.

Mystical Reawakenings

A glimmer in the broken night,
Ancient stars align,
In the silence, pure delight,
Old magics intertwine.

Dust of ages, spirits surge,
From crypts long locked away,
Wisps of light in swift converge,
To greet the dawning day.

Incantations, soft and clear,
With moonlit shadows sway,
Awakens whispers we hold dear,
Where timeless forces play.

From the depths of lore long past,
New enchantments rise,
Reviving truths that ever last,
Beneath enchanted skies.

Through the veil, the mortal sees,
The ageless powers blend,
On the whispered evening breeze,
Infinite magics lend.

The Revival of Ancient Energies

Veins of earth, pure power flows,
Through ancient roots and stone,
From forgotten hollows grows,
A might once softly known.

Elements in sacred bind,
Renew the spirit's force,
An echo from the dawn of time,
Charting a hidden course.

Sacred fire, winds of night,
The waters deep and old,
Energies of primal might,
In mysteries unfold.

Through the cosmic tether's spin,
Revival's essence starts,
Reawakening from within,
The rhythm of our hearts.

Starlit pathways, spirits call,
In rituals, we're found,
Ancient energies enthrall,
In their eternal round.

The Rediscovery of Sorcery

Beneath forgotten tomes of lore,
A whisper softly stirs,
In shadows where old magics soar,
The sorcerer's chant recurs.

Candles flicker, shadows play,
In circles carved in stone,
Revealing secrets of the fey,
Where mystic winds have blown.

Elixirs brewed in moonlight's gleam,
Potions potent, rare,
Reviving long-forgotten dreams,
Suspended in the air.

Spells inscribed on pages thin,
Runes of ethereal flight,
In the twilight, we begin,
A voyage through the night.

In cryptic symbols, power traced,
Beyond the realms we see,
With ancient arts, we are embraced,
By sorcery, set free.

Reclaiming Sorcerous Strength

In shadows deep, where whispers cling,
A mage reborn in twilight's ring,
Reclaiming strength that dusk forgot,
A soul unbound from time's own knot.

Arcane embers, fiercely bright,
Illuminate the darkest night,
With every spell, a pulse of life,
Unraveling the threads of strife.

The ancient tome, with pages worn,
Its secrets speak of powers sworn,
A wizard stands on destiny's brink,
From the abyss, he shall not sink.

Mystic winds around him coil,
Binding fate in magic's toil,
His heart alight with endless might,
Reclaiming strength, his given right.

In realms beyond where dreams convene,
He walks the paths of unseen sheen,
A sorcerer, where strength is king,
In shadows deep, where whispers cling.

The Enchanter's Resurgence

In the quiet of the crescent moon,
An enchanter stirs, his powers tune,
Resurgence flows through veins anew,
With ancient sage, and morning dew.

When stars align in silent song,
The magic dormant, now feels strong,
With gestures known and words precise,
He conjures dreams from realms of ice.

Forgotten spells from ages past,
Through him, the mystic light is cast,
Revival blooms in every spree,
In the enchanter's quest for spree.

His wand alights with cosmic force,
Guiding him on his true course,
No shadow deep can hide the thrall,
Of resurgence, answering his call.

With whispered chants in twilight's gleam,
He walks the edges of the dream,
An enchanter's power reborn grand,
Commanding magic's vast expanse.

Awakened

From slumber deep the soul now wakes,
In sunrise hues, the dawn remakes,
A spirit freed from night's embrace,
To find its path, a new-found grace.

With eyes that gleam like starlit skies,
Awakened heart, no longer lies,
From depths of dreams, it rises tall,
Against the night's oppressive thrall.

Through forests thick and meadows wide,
It dances forth with ancient pride,
In every breath, a whisper sings,
Of freedom's gift and open wings.

The past dissolves in morning's ray,
New journeys start with each new day,
Awakened, now, with purpose clear,
To chase the dreams that linger near.

In realms where sunshine meets the sea,
It finds the strength to just be free,
Awakened soul with light entwined,
To touch the skies by fate assigned.

Phoenix of Arcane

From ashes cold, the phoenix springs,
On fiery dawn and blazing wings,
Reborn in magic's tender flame,
It takes once more an arcane name.

Through mysteries of night it soared,
Untangling spells in waves it roared,
The arcane pulse within its core,
Guided by the lore of yore.

Each feather held a tale untold,
Of secrets ancient, brave, and bold,
With every flight, it forged the path,
Through trials fierce, through sorcerous wrath.

In skies where shadows tremble near,
The phoenix's cry was bright and clear,
A beacon of enchanted light,
That pushed against the brooding night.

From flames of dusk to dawn's rebirth,
It spreads its magic through the earth,
Phoenix of the arcane rise,
An eternal fire against the skies.

Unveiling Hidden Charms

In shadows deep, where secrets lie,
A world unfolds to curious eyes,
Gems of wonder, masked in calm,
Await the touch of unveiled charms.

With every step, a mystery cleaves,
To those who seek, the heart believes,
Whispers linger in twilight's arms,
As night reveals its hidden charms.

An earthly scent, both fresh and old,
Tales of love and dreams untold,
Boundless grace where beauty swarms,
In every soul, a hidden charm.

The moonlit path, a silver quilt,
Woven tales of joy and guilt,
Wrap your spirit in warmth and balm,
For life unveils its hidden charms.

With heart and mind, explore the lanes,
Where peace and chaos ever reigns,
In every tear, in all alarm,
We find, at last, life's hidden charms.

Reigniting the Arcane Flame

From ashes cold, the embers rise,
A phoenix born of ancient skies,
Through trials fierce and battles tame,
We reignite the arcane flame.

A spark of hope, a kindle's grace,
Unseen powers in hidden space,
With rhythms older than a name,
Revive the lost, the arcane flame.

Through shadows cast in moonlit haze,
Unveil the light of brighter days,
A spell of old, none can defame,
Eternally burns the arcane flame.

In chants of old, lies wisdom pure,
In heartbeats rare, a mystic cure,
Mysteries come, none are the same,
Yet all shall heed the arcane flame.

Together, we will stoke the fire,
With every wish and pure desire,
In unity, we play the game,
And guard the light, the arcane flame.

The Spirit's Magic Regained

A soul once lost in twilight's dust,
In shadows gray and vacant lust,
Now seeks the light, heart unchained,
The spirit's magic thus regained.

With every dawn, a chance anew,
A spark of joy in morning's dew,
Through valleys dark, through fields unstained,
The spirit's magic is regained.

In whispered winds of ancient lore,
Find strength within, forevermore,
For in each trial, the truth ordained,
The spirit's magic is regained.

With hands outstretched to skies so wide,
Embrace the world with newfound pride,
In every step, a past refrained,
The spirit's magic is regained.

Together, we shall walk this path,
Through storm and peace, through gentlest wrath,
In union strong, unfeigned, unfeigned,
Our spirits' magic thus regained.

Mending Broken Enchantments

In shards of dreams where hopes have gone,
We weave the thread from ancient dawn,
To heal the wounds, to bridge the rants,
In mending broken enchantments.

A heart once torn by fleeting time,
In verses strong, we seek to rhyme,
The pieces burn, but now they dance,
Mending broken enchantments.

With every tear, a mystic glow,
In every pain, a healing flow,
For in the cracks, we take our stance,
And mend the broken enchantments.

In whispers soft, in voices true,
In shades of old, in skies anew,
We find the love, the second chance,
To mend the broken enchantments.

Together now, we cast the spells,
In unity, our spirit swells,
To build anew from circumstance,
The mended broken enchantments.

Awakening My Twilight Charms

Under the glow of twilight's veil,
Secrets whisper, tales regale,
With every star, a hidden gem,
Reviving ancient diadem.

Winds caress the silent night,
Moonlit paths, a guiding light,
In shadows deep, my spirit warms,
Awakening my twilight charms.

Dew-kissed grass beneath my tread,
Mystic wonders gently spread,
Each step echoes through the calm,
Invoking spells like soothing balm.

Lucid dreams in darkness spun,
Together, they become as one,
Enchanted realms, where magic swarms,
Awakening my twilight charms.

The Return of the Essence

Whispers of the dawn arise,
In the stillness, no disguise,
Essence long lost, draws near,
Filling hearts with vibrant cheer.

Old roots grasp the earth anew,
Memories in morning dew,
Infinite threads of life restore,
Essence found forevermore.

Sunlit beams on rivers dance,
Mark the seamless circumstance,
Where time's tapestry will blend,
The essence starts to mend.

Eyes alight with spirit's fire,
Breath by breath, we climb higher,
Into skies, past earthly cairns,
The return of the essence soars.

Weaving the Thread of Spells

In the loom of moonlit hours,
Threads of fate, our hidden powers,
Weave a tapestry of day,
Charmed by night in intricate play.

Whispering winds through nature's loom,
Crafting spells in twilight's gloom,
With each stitch, the magic swells,
Weaving the thread of ancient spells.

Ethereal hues blend soft and bright,
Symbols dance in silver light,
Hands move deftly, stories tell,
Boundless secrets time shall compel.

From dusk till dawn we intertwine,
Mysteries in each design,
A timeless weave that fate compels,
Weaving the thread of endless spells.

Harvesting Stardust Dreams

Beneath the vault of midnight skies,
Dreamers wander, spirits rise,
Gathering stardust's gentle gleams,
From celestial beams.

Each spark a wish, a yearning true,
Caught within the morning dew,
With every whisper, hope redeems,
Harvesting those stardust dreams.

Twilight shimmers, soft and bright,
Guides us through the velvet night,
Into the seas of cosmic streams,
Afloat on endless stardust dreams.

In the quiet, seeds take hold,
Future tales in light enfold,
Thus, we carry, hope that seams,
Harvesting our stardust dreams.

Spellbound Restoration

In the quiet still of twilight's weave,
Whispers of the old world retrieve.
Nature's symphony softly roars,
As magic breathes through ancient doors.

Echoes blend in the forest deep,
Where shadows hold the secrets they keep.
A murmured incantation flows,
Reviving life where enchantment grows.

Rivers carve their timeless path,
Revitalizing souls with a secret bath.
Earth and sky in harmony sing,
An age-old dance in an endless ring.

Mystic winds through branches sigh,
Touching heaven with a solemn cry.
Nature mends its sacred crest
In the heart of wilderness, we rest.

Lingering light at dusk's end,
Hails a spell that time can't rend.
Restored by the whispering trees,
Our spirits find eternal ease.

Eclipsing the Mundane

Under a sky of woven night,
Stars unfold their silent flight.
Moonbeams dance in silver grace,
Eclipsing the mundane's embrace.

A journey starts with a hidden sign,
Through cosmic seas to realms divine.
Mysteries shroud the path untold,
Where wonders bloom in stories bold.

City lights fade to distant gleam,
Reality melts into a dream.
Boundless skies and endless streams,
Guide us through this world of seams.

In moments brief, infinity rides,
As we traverse the starry tides.
Magic found in every shade,
Where heaven and earth serenade.

When morning's touch renews the day,
Ethereal whispers start to fray.
Yet, memories of the night remain,
Eclipsing the mundane again.

The Enchantment Reclaimed

Through ancient halls where whispers tread,
Into the heart where stories are fed.
Lost enchantments call our name,
Implore us now, their power reclaim.

Veins of light in darkness lace,
Illuminating each hidden trace.
Arcane symbols, silent plea,
Unlock the realms of mystery.

Tales of yore, forgotten lore,
Awaiting those who dare explore.
Beyond the veil of mortal sight,
Magic reclaims its ancient right.

Echoes linger through the time,
Resonating with a secret rhyme.
In silence, truth shall be proclaimed,
Ancient spells are soon reclaimed.

Our souls once dormant now awake,
With every step, the past we take.
Enchanted paths our spirits frame,
In this world, we reclaim the flame.

Finding the Mystic Pulse

In twilight's calm, where shadows fall,
The essence of the earth's last call.
Nature's heart imparts its beat,
Finding the pulse beneath our feet.

Through woven glade and crystal springs,
Life's raw magic gently sings.
Passengers in this sacred trust,
Ashes rise, return to dust.

Stars above, their light imparts,
Secrets of the cosmic charts.
Silent hints of hidden force,
Guide us on our destined course.

Whispers in the moonlit air,
Envelop us with a tender care.
Time's fabric sways in gentle burst,
To know the pulse, we must submerse.

Paths of light and shadow mix,
The mystic pulse—our minds affix.
In seeking we, the soul's true source,
Embrace at last, the universe.

Awakening Celestial Powers

In the quiet depths of night,
Stars ignite their ancient gleam,
Dreamers find a guiding light,
Lost in an ethereal dream.

Galaxies in spiral dance,
Mysteries unfold afar,
Every wish taken a chance,
In the heart of every star.

Wisdom in the cosmic swirl,
Signs written in the skies,
Hearts of sage and every girl,
Hear the universe's cries.

Constellations paint the tale,
Lonely souls in search of grace,
Through the void and silver veil,
They encounter their own pace.

Morning comes with burning hues,
Solstice whispering in ears,
Godly power we must use,
Vanquishing our primal fears.

Redeeming the Lost Charm

Through the shadows, seek the light,
Every charm deserves a chance,
Whisper softly to the night,
Reignite the sacred dance.

Broken spells and fractured hearts,
Gathered pieces, dust and gold,
Forge anew what once departs,
Of lost magic tales retold.

Crystals gleam beneath the moon,
Hidden secrets they unveil,
Ancient runes begin to tune,
Songs of yore they loudly hail.

Hope returns in steady waves,
Strengthened by a found delight,
Every trial a soul it saves,
In this ever-binding night.

Now the charm is pure and strong,
Guarded by the stars that gleam,
Bound to right what once was wrong,
Dreamers sail on morn's first beam.

Enchantress Rising

In the forest old and wise,
Mystics cast their hopeful gaze,
From the depths where shadows rise,
Magic born of ancient days.

Echoes of a whispered spell,
Carry through the twilight air,
In her hands, the power dwells,
Crafted from the purest care.

Glimmering with dusk's embrace,
She ascends in softest hue,
Every star reflects her grace,
As the night her spirit grew.

Nature bows to her command,
Waves of light and dark entwine,
Mountains, seas, obey her hand,
Ebb and flow by her design.

Rising on the eastern breeze,
Freedom in her eyes does gleam,
With her touch, the world at ease,
Enchantress now fulfills her dream.

The Warlock's Regain

Lost in shadows deep and cold,
Power yielded to the night,
Subtle threads of stories told,
Lead him back to dawn's first light.

Through the mazes of the dark,
Ancient whispers guide his quest,
Every star a guiding spark,
Luring him to fortune's crest.

Magic faltered, magic lost,
Binds now broken in the past,
Hearts and spirits count the cost,
Yet his will remains steadfast.

Healing words and potions brewed,
By his hands redemption made,
Secrets of the earth renewed,
In the twilight's gentle shade.

Now with strength and wisdom gained,
Warlock stands with power anew,
Energy no longer strained,
Magic's flame forever true.

Remembering the Sorceress

In the shadows of her whispers,
Mysteries weave and twist,
Eyes that glimpse the ancient lore,
Hands that shape the mist.

Her laughter circles moonlit nights,
Enchanting all who hear,
From the cauldron's bubbling depths,
Arises both joy and fear.

A wisp of smoke, a fleeting star,
She dances through the dark,
With every chant and whispered spell,
She leaves a lasting mark.

Beneath the ancient willow trees,
Her spirit still remains,
In moonlit glades and secret waves,
Her magic soars and reigns.

Forever shall we seek her trail,
In dreams and silent loves,
Remembering the sorceress,
Who walks the stars above.

Bloom of Magic Within

From seeds of dreams and silken thoughts,
A magic garden grows,
With petals bright and stories old,
Its beauty ever shows.

In every heart, a mystic bloom,
A spell of pure desire,
To light the paths with shimmering hope,
And set the soul on fire.

Cherish the bloom within your soul,
It whispers through the night,
With colors that defy the dark,
And bring the dawn to light.

Embrace the magic deep inside,
Let it take root and grow,
For in the silent secret hours,
Its strength begins to show.

In every life, a garden thrives,
With blossoms strange and rare,
The bloom of magic lies within,
Beyond the realms of care.

Vibrant Sorcery Reimagined

In twilight's hues, a vivid spell,
A world beyond the known,
With colors bright and shadows deep,
Its wonders brightly shown.

The sorcery of ancient times,
Reimagined, reborn,
In tales where dragons dance and fly,
And heroes find the morn.

Magic pulses through the air,
In every whispered breeze,
Where castles float on clouds of dreams,
Above enchanted seas.

Craft your spells with heart and hand,
Let imagination soar,
For in the vibrant tapestry,
Lie secrets evermore.

The future's spell is in our grasp,
A vibrant sorcery,
Reimagined through our dreams and hopes,
A boundless, wild decree.

Return to the Mystic Realm

Through veils of time, the path unwinds,
To realms of ancient lore,
Where spirits drift on twilight winds,
And magic's heart can soar.

In misty glens and shadowed vales,
The mystic portal calls,
To wander through enchanted woods,
By streams and mossy walls.

With every step, the air grows thick,
With echoes of the past,
The whispering of fallen leaves,
A spell that's ever cast.

Return to where the magic lives,
In places old and wild,
Where moonbeams light the sacred groves,
And wisdom speaks, beguiled.

From this ancient, mystic realm,
New dreams and visions stem,
And in our hearts, it lies again,
The land of our return.

The Reclaimed Wizardry

In shadows deep, where secrets lie,
Old spells awaken by moon's cry,
Once lost, now found in mystic night,
The wizard's power sparks to flight.

Ancient books with runes they bind,
Unlock the magic of the mind,
Hands aloft, with stars aligned,
A realm of wonders redefined.

Whispers echo, timeless chant,
Arcane winds through fingers grant,
Sorcery's return, defiant stand,
Mysteries held within the hand.

Forgotten incantations flow,
Through ether's dance, the magic show,
Revived from dust and time's decay,
The wizard rules where shadows play.

In twilight's glow, the old and new,
Spellcraft bind in twilight's hue,
Sorcerous strength, once lost, now found,
The wizard's might, forever crowned.

Arcane Persistence

In ancient halls where whispers fade,
A spark ignites, and shadows wade,
Through years of silence, dark and cold,
Arcane persistence, brave and bold.

The mage, with eyes like burning coal,
Reclaims the secrets, makes them whole,
A tapestry of mystic lore,
With every spell, the magic soars.

Through storm and sun, the trials faced,
A spirit fierce, no time to waste,
With every chant, with every call,
The mage defies, he stands tall.

In runes and glyphs, the power found,
The mage's voice, a timeless sound,
Beyond the realms of mortal gaze,
Arcane persistence lights the blaze.

Through labyrinths of endless night,
The mage ascends in mystic flight,
From ashes risen, bound by fate,
The arcane's might, never too late.

The Mage's Revival Journey

Through mirrored realms and twilight's seam,
The mage sets forth, where shadows gleam,
A path entwined with fate's own string,
A journey's start for magic's king.

With staff in hand, and heart of steel,
The wizard seeks what world conceals,
Through ancient gates and whispered spells,
The mage's quest where magic dwells.

In forests deep and oceans wide,
Through realms unseen, the mage will glide,
Reviving strength, renewing grace,
A quest for truth in endless space.

With every step, the powers grow,
Revival breathes where winds may blow,
On distant peaks and valleys deep,
The mage's journey will not sleep.

The stars align, the cosmos sings,
Unlocking ancient, hallowed strings,
A saga told in timeless lore,
The mage's journey, forever more.

Sorcerous Revival

Beneath the moon's ethereal light,
Darkened realms give way to sight,
Sorcerer's breath, the night fulfills,
A power reborn in ancient hills.

From ashes cold, the flames arise,
A mystic force through tear-filled eyes,
Old runes speak of times once lost,
A sorcerer reclaims at any cost.

The skies aglow with arcane fire,
Reviving dreams of lost desire,
With whispered words and casting hand,
Sorcerer's magic sweeps the land.

In every wave of spectral gleam,
The sorcerer revives the dream,
A legacy, reborn and bright,
Carving paths through endless night.

Where shadows stretched and doubts did creep,
Sorcerer's vows, forever to keep,
Revived in strength with heart anew,
In mystic realms where legends grew.

Restoring Hidden Talismans

In the depths of forgotten air,
Lie secrets, myths, beyond repair;
Whispered charms in shadows cast,
Old talismans, bound to last.

Through time's weave, and ages' rust,
We find the gold, dissolve the dust;
Ancient scripts, in moonlight veil,
Histories tucked within our trail.

Eyes attuned to what is lost,
Wander through the seasons' frost;
Echoes cling to heart and mind,
Hidden truths, the soul will find.

Gems of wisdom, faint and rare,
Shine anew with tender care;
Veiled in subtle, quiet breath,
Talismans defy their death.

With each touch, the past restores,
Unlocking whispers through closed doors;
In these treasures, life expands,
Guidance found in timeless hands.

The Arcane Phoenix

Beneath the twilight's dusky veil,
A legend wakes in whispered tale;
Feathers weave through embered sky,
Arcane Phoenix soars on high.

Born from ashes, flamed anew,
Ancient secrets burning through;
Rising through the midnight's song,
Where hidden magics grow most strong.

Molten shadows, vibrant plume,
Illuminates the night's deep gloom;
Cycle endless, life reborn,
Embraced within the night and morn.

Each rebirth, a purer form,
Weathering each stormy swarm;
Timeless wisdom in each glow,
Nature's heart in fire flow.

As dawn approaches, skies ignite,
Unveiling wings in radiant flight;
Phoenix, guardian of lore,
Eternal flame forevermore.

Resurrecting the Inner Magus

Inside the stillness of the mind,
Lies ancient power, bound and kind;
Veins of magic, coursing through,
Wisdom seeking form anew.

Silent whispers, dreams provoked,
In corners dim, the fire stoked;
Inner magus calls to rise,
Embrace the mystic, clear your eyes.

Elements in harmony,
Resurrect the symphony;
In deep meditation's trance,
Lost incantations find their dance.

Unveil the cloak of hidden fears,
Draw upon the lunar spheres;
Ancient echoes feed the light,
Inner magus aids your flight.

Through the realms of waking thought,
Alchemy of soul is sought;
Resurrect, transform, attain,
Inner magus, break the chain.

Arcane Blossom

In gardens where the shadows fall,
Whispers speak of ancient lore,
A flower blooms, majestic, tall,
Its secrets bound forevermore.

Petals gleam with hues unknown,
Magic in its every vein,
From dusk till dawn it's brightly shown,
Mystic beauty in the rain.

Guarded by the moonlit tide,
Winds of fate will brush its face,
In its scent, the stars confide,
Binding time in soft embrace.

Riddles wrapped within its core,
Blooming in the silent night,
Arcane forces, evermore,
In the blossom's gentle light.

Wand's Whisper

In the still of twilight's breath,
Wand in hand, the mage can hear,
Mystic whispers, conquering death,
Echoes from a world so near.

Wood entwined with runes of gold,
Power ancient, wisdom's might,
Tales of ages yet untold,
Hidden in the fading light.

Listen, as the wand reveals,
Destinies both dark and bright,
Secrets bound in arcane seals,
Vanishing with morning's light.

Whispers float on evening air,
Touched by magic, purely kind,
In the wand's embrace, beware,
Mysteries that baffle mind.

Shamanic Renewal

In the heart of forest deep,
Ancient chants begin to rise,
Wandering minds, they do seep,
Calling spirits from the skies.

Drums of earth, a primal beat,
Echo through the sacred glen,
Feet of wisdom take the heat,
Shaman's voice, beyond the ken.

With the wind in firm embrace,
Roots entwine with tales of old,
Healing hands do interlace,
Mending souls with touch of gold.

Cycles turn and life does spin,
Phoenix rises, reborn anew,
Shaman's song, within, begins,
Breaking dawn with wisdom's hue.

The Magician's Reclamation

Beneath the stars of midnight's dome,
A magician stands alone,
Casting spells from ancient tome,
In a voice of somber tone.

Lost in realms of eldritch power,
Seeking truths that few have seen,
Claiming back the midnight hour,
In a world of lost, unclean.

Wisdom reclaimed, his heart now pure,
Divine light in eyes of old,
Fate and magic, they endure,
Stories of the lost retold.

In the dawn, his path set straight,
Harnessed by a newfound might,
Wielding power, he awaits,
Reclaimed magic in the night.

Potent Powers Restored

In shadows deep, where secrets lie,
A whispering wind begins to sigh,
Ancient runes, upon the floor,
Potent powers are restored.

A flicker of light, a spark of life,
Cutting through the endless strife,
A circle drawn, a spell transferred,
Potent powers are restored.

Hands raise high, chants resound,
Mystic forces all around,
Veins imbued, with magic stored,
Potent powers are restored.

Eyes open wide, the world a glint,
Legends rise from ancient print,
Hear the call, heed the word,
Potent powers are restored.

Through the veil, truth explored,
Cosmic fate now underscored,
Epic tales to be unfurled,
Potent powers are restored.

The Magus Reborn

In the still of midnight's core,
A figure steps through ancient lore,
Robes of twilight, staff adorned,
Behold, the Magus reborn.

Stars align, their pattern clear,
Echoes from a yesteryear,
Elements by will transformed,
Behold, the Magus reborn.

Mountains bow, rivers bend,
Realms redefine and transcend,
Waking dreams and futures formed,
Behold, the Magus reborn.

Circles drawn in sacred sand,
Wisdom gripped within his hand,
Timeless truths by magic sworn,
Behold, the Magus reborn.

Through the ages, dark to light,
Guarding realms from endless night,
A destiny that can't be scorned,
Behold, the Magus reborn.

Rebirth of the Enigma

Silent whispers, hidden shades,
Cryptic paths through time's cascades,
From the void, the mists perform,
The rebirth of the enigma forms.

Ciphers locked in shadows deep,
Awaken from their coded sleep,
Minds entangled, theories swarm,
The rebirth of the enigma forms.

Eyes perceive the unseen thread,
Lingering where the wise have tread,
Mysteries both cold and warm,
The rebirth of the enigma forms.

Translucent masks, stories spun,
Until the night and day are one,
Real and false distinctions blurred,
The rebirth of the enigma heard.

Infinite realms within one thought,
Paths to truths are fiercely sought,
In darkened haze where light is born,
The rebirth of the enigma forms.

Celestial Reawakening

Cosmos whisper, stars ignite,
Celestial paths of purest light,
In the silence, chaos breaking,
Begins the celestial reawakening.

Planets pulse with newfound grace,
Comets race in timeless chase,
Galaxies in dance partaking,
Behold the celestial reawakening.

Nebulas in colors blaze,
Eternal in their cosmic maze,
From the void, systems waking,
Sign of celestial reawakening.

Auroras weave across the night,
Radiant with ethereal might,
In their glow, futures making,
Signal the celestial reawakening.

'Cross the skies, a dawn reborn,
Heralding an endless morn,
Epoch ends, new dawn staking,
Witness the celestial reawakening.

The Sorcerer's Rediscovery

In ancient tomes, the magic sleeps,
A whispering of times gone by.
The sorcerer, through shadows, creeps,
Unveiling secrets to the sky.

Forgotten spells in dust emerge,
With power humming in the air.
The arcane currents start to surge,
A dance of fire everywhere.

The runes once lost, now found again,
They glow with otherworldly light.
The sorcerer, with might and pen,
Writes destinies within the night.

Unlocking doors of realms unseen,
Where myths and legends freely roam.
The fabric of the night serene,
Holds stories seeking to come home.

And in the heart of twilight's breath,
The magic knows no bounds nor clime.
The sorcerer defies the death,
Transcending both the space and time.

Renewed Wizardry

Upon the hill where twilight dwells,
The wizard's power reawakens.
With chants that weave through ancient wells,
The spirit of the past is shaken.

A staff in hand, a cloak of night,
He draws symbols in the air.
Lost relics in the moon's soft light,
Reveal their secrets rare and fair.

The stars align, the ether hums,
The wizard speaks in tongues arcane.
The river of enchantment runs,
And magic courses through each vein.

Forgotten arts, reborn anew,
The winds of fate begin to shift.
In colors vivid, bold, and true,
The world receives his wondrous gift.

With every breath, creation sings,
A symphony of spells and lore.
The wizard spreads his shadowed wings,
Redefining evermore.

Mystique Rekindled

Beneath the stars where secrets keep,
A new dawn rises, mystique bright.
The embers of the past now leap,
Igniting through the spellbound night.

The wizard's gaze, both wise and deep,
Sees pathways hidden from the eye.
With ancient chants, the shadows sweep,
Across the realms where spirits fly.

A fire once dimmed, now fiercely burns,
In the cauldron of his soul.
The wheel of fate again it turns,
With magic as its guiding pole.

Enigmas dance upon the flame,
The runes recall their timeless song.
A world reborn, yet still the same,
Where right and wrong no longer throng.

Mystique rekindled, sparks the night,
The wizard claims his place once more.
In every spell cast in the light,
An echo from the days of yore.

Returning the Mystic Flame

From ashes of the arcane lore,
The flame of magic starts anew.
The wizard walks the ancient floor,
With eyes that see beyond the blue.

A torch alight with wondrous fire,
He carries through the veils of time.
Each step revealing one desire,
To master realms both grand and prime.

With whispers old, incantations fly,
The mystic threads begin to weave.
A tapestry of stars drawn nigh,
By hands that once the gods believed.

An altar holds the mystic flame,
Eternal in its burning bright.
Its flicker speaks the wizard's name,
A beacon in the endless night.

So, past and future intertwine,
In cycles of the old and new.
The mystic flame, it shall define,
The magic that he must pursue.

Rediscovering the Sorcerer Within

In the quiet night, a stir inside
Magic whispers where shadows hide
The moon's soft gleam, a guiding light
Awakens spells from ancient night

Forgotten tomes with pages worn
Secrets, spells, by daylight sworn
Echoes of a power grand
Enchantment woven by thy hand

Through mist and fog, the path revealed
A power latent, once concealed
Within the heart, a sorcerer's might
To once again embrace the night

Stars align, the world in bloom
Breaking free from endless gloom
Rediscover the wizard's song
A journey back where you belong

With staff and wand, with heart so true
The magic, now, belongs to you
Embrace it now, the past reprise
The sorcerer within your eyes

The Return of Wonder

Beneath the stars, where dreams ignite
A spark returns within the night
An ancient call, a whispered name
Recalling joy, forsaking shame

In every leaf, in every bough
A timeless magic whispers how
To see the world through eyes reborn
And greet the glow of every morn

A childlike gaze revives within
A heart that's new, where we begin
To seek the marvels near and far
In distant land or twinkling star

With every step on paths untold
New wonders bloom, new tales unfold
A treasure trove of endless light
Where mystery brings sweet delight

Return once more to realms of old
Where every moment turns to gold
Let wonder's flame again befriend
For magic's touch shall never end

Rekindling the Spark Inside

In stillness lies a dormant fire
A latent dream, a quiet desire
With gentle breath, the embers flare
Rekindling hope, dissolving despair

Through trials dark, through shadows grim
A light persists, though faint and dim
A single spark, a boundless flame
To rise anew, to stake a claim

Within the heart, a secret song
Played soft and true, though silent long
Awaits the moment to reprise
The melody of bright sunrise

From ashes old, a phoenix high
Ascends the vault of sapphire sky
To burn anew with fervor bright
Illuminating darkest night

Rebirth of strength, a soul on fire
With passion's blaze, it climbs higher
In every heartbeat, dreams reside
Rekindling the spark inside

Courageous Mysticism Renewed

In twilight's embrace, brave hearts ignite,
Mystical shadows, dancing in night.
Courage reborn within the veil,
Embarking on tales, ancient and frail.

Stars whisper secrets through cosmic tide,
In realms where mystics and dreams collide.
Courage to seek beyond the seen,
Awaits in places where souls convene.

A chalice in hand, inscribed with lore,
Ancient whispers open the door.
To bravery found in silent alchemy,
Where spirit meets with harmony.

An owl's gaze, a cryptic guide,
Through courage mystic, none need hide.
Renounce the fog of earthly doubt,
In the ritual dance, let mystics shout.

The heart grows strong on paths anew,
With courage in mysticism's hue.
Reborn, refreshed, by stars aligned,
A journey of spirit and mind.

Aura of Reclaimed Wonder

In dawn's first light, a sense awakes,
To realms of wonder, soul partakes.
Aura reclaimed in morning's breath,
Life's wonder blooms, defying death.

A field of dreams where asters glow,
In twilight whispers, spirits flow.
Reclaimed are sights of distant shores,
As wonder's magic swiftly soars.

In every leaf, a tale untold,
The aura of the brave and bold.
With eyes reborn, and heart renewed,
To ancient wonders, we're pursued.

Mysteries weave in golden hue,
Of skies where night and day construe.
Reclaiming wonder in each gaze,
A path where spirit truly stays.

Embrace the aura, sought and found,
In nature's beauty, all around.
With wonder, journey through the door,
To realms of wonder, evermore.

Whispers of the Phoenix Wand

In ashes cold, new life deceived,
By phoenix wand, the world reprieved.
Whispers fly on wings of dawn,
Rising sun, past gloom withdrawn.

Flames return to form anew,
A cycle of wonders to pursue.
Whispered secrets, ancient told,
In phoenix's grip, life behold.

The silent wand, with power pure,
In hands of fate, enduring sure.
With whispers soft in twilight's bond,
Life reignites from phoenix wand.

Through trials burnt, the soul shall rise,
By spectral wand 'neath beaming skies.
From embers bright, new paths respond,
To whispers of the phoenix wand.

Eternal flight through tempests high,
Rebirth in whispers, never die.
The wand, a beacon, life beyond,
In every heart, a phoenix fond.

The Magician's Comeback

In shadows deep where secrets lie,
A magician's power, none deny.
With incantations, stars align,
Ancient arts in hands divine.

The wand returns to rightful place,
In practiced hands, a sacred space.
With every flick, the cosmos bends,
In magic's flow, no bitter ends.

Curtains rise on grand display,
Where mysteries dance and shadows sway.
The comeback tale of ageless lore,
Revived in spells, forevermore.

Illusions break, as light inclines,
The magician's craft, in subtle signs.
Return of one who bends the night,
In arcane ways, where soul takes flight.

Through mirrored halls and twilight maze,
The magician marks the world's praise.
Comeback strong to realms unknown,
In magic's art, forever shown.

The Mage's Awakening

Within the silent night, the stars align,
Mystic whispers, the arcane signs,
A mage awakens, magic is nigh,
Waves of power, lift to the sky.

Ancient tomes, secrets reveal,
The essence of magic, a power to feel,
Runes are drawn, incantations spoken,
Worlds unseen, the veil is broken.

Light and shadow, dance as one,
The spell is cast, destiny begun,
Elements bow, to the mage's command,
Infinite realms, in the palm of a hand.

From depths unknown, strength revives,
The mage's spirit, once more thrives,
Etheric energies, flow through veins,
Breaking free from forgotten chains.

The dawn approaches, horizons break,
The mage's powers fully awake,
A journey starts, through realms untold,
With wisdom ancient, courage bold.

Rediscovered Enchantment

In the heart of an old, silent grove,
Whispers of magic, the winds wove,
Forgotten charms, in shadows hid,
Rediscovered enchantment, beneath the lid.

Ancient trees, with secrets to share,
Their leaves whisper, tales in the air,
A touch of magic, serenity found,
Spells awaken, within the ground.

Crystals gleam, beneath the night,
Mystic glow in the soft moonlight,
Enchanted whispers, through the glen,
Magic reborn, where dreams begin.

Emerald earth, with a sacred sheen,
Revives enchantment, once unseen,
Nature's melody, an old refrain,
Magic discovered, in the rain.

In this grove, where time stands still,
The essence of magic, pure and real,
Ancient powers, once misplaced,
Rediscovered enchantment, now embraced.

Arcane Resurrection

Beneath the stars, a ritual starts,
Ancient magic, from silent hearts,
A resurrection of powers long passed,
Waking the arcane, a spell is cast.

Elements gather, a cosmic dance,
Reviving the old, a second chance,
Chanting hymns, in shadows deep,
Awakening secrets, once in sleep.

The earth trembles, a pulse renewed,
Arcane forces, askew then accrued,
From hidden realms, magic ascends,
Resurrected truth, the air transcends.

Time unwinds, revealing the past,
Spirits rise, from the shadows cast,
Ancient circles, drawn in sand,
Arcane rebirth within the land.

With power unfurled, destinies realigned,
Arcane energies, forever intertwined,
An endless cycle, never undone,
Resurrected magic, twilight begun.

The Shaman's Path Reclaimed

Through forests deep and mountains grand,
A shaman steps, staff in hand,
Echoes of wisdom, ancient yore,
Paths of old, he will explore.

Spirits guide him, through night and day,
In the sacred dance, he sways,
Ritual chants, from lips that know,
Reclaiming knowledge, from long ago.

With every step, the land he heals,
Nature's truth, again he feels,
Totems rise, in twilight's gleam,
Awakening power, in a dream.

The spirits' whispers, gentle and clear,
Through gusts of wind, shaman will hear,
Mystic paths, once more tread,
Ancient bonds, mended and spread.

In harmony with earth, sky, and sea,
The shaman's path, reclaimed and free,
Binding the sacred, to realms untamed,
The shaman's journey, fully claimed.

Renewed by Ancient Whispers

Under the canopy of yesteryears, I tread,
Whispers of old haunt the path ahead.
Through leaves that cradle forgotten lore,
I find myself where ages pour.

Timeless voices, gentle, wise,
Speak of the cycles, the lows, the highs.
Their echoes swirl in the evening air,
Gifting wisdom beyond compare.

The rivers murmur secrets untold,
Of firelight stories, forever bold.
In silent nights and moonlit beams,
I see the stars carry age-old dreams.

Awakened by songs from twilight's rim,
I trace the lines of an ancient hymn.
Where shadows of past and present meet,
I walk into the whispers, bittersweet.

In the heart of echoes, I find my name,
Renewed by whispers, I'm never the same.
Carved by time, yet born anew,
In ancient whispers, my spirit grew.

The Sorcerer's Dawn

At the break of dawn, spells unfold,
Crafted in twilight, whispers bold.
A sorcerer's chant, both low and high,
Weaves through the canvas of the sky.

Mystic sighs in the morning air,
With a flick of light, magic is there.
Golden beams and shadows blend,
In dawn's embrace, incantations send.

The forest awakens with every spell,
Leaves and echoes in a mystic swell.
Creatures of twilight stir and rise,
Amidst the morning's sorcery lies.

On the horizon, a wizard's gaze,
Crafts new hope in dawn's blaze.
With every word, the day begins,
A sorcerer's dawn, where magic wins.

Through each sunrise, the world reborn,
In silence broken by ancient horn.
With conjured dreams, the light is drawn,
Blessed by the Sorcerer's dawn.

Flickers of My Lost Enchantment

In the dim corners, where dreams converge,
Flickers of enchantment softly surge.
Once boundless magic, now a fleeting glow,
Like ashes of a fire long ago.

Echoes of spells that once were bright,
Wane in the stillness of the night.
Breaths of wonder find their way,
Through memories of a brighter day.

Shadows of glories from realms unseen,
Dance upon the edges of what has been.
In every flicker, a fragment gleams,
Of woven spells and broken dreams.

Whispers of power, faint but clear,
Remind me of the magic near.
In the twilight, I search and yearn,
For enchantments lost, to once return.

Among the flickers, I reclaim,
Fragments of a once great flame.
In lost enchantment, hope is found,
And magic anew begins to sound.

The Rebirth of Mystical Power

Beneath the stars, in twilight's veil,
Mystical power begins to trail.
In shadows deep and moonlit hours,
Awakens ancient, dormant powers.

From the ashes of forgotten lands,
Sorcery rises, and magic stands.
With chants unspoken, long confined,
New spells in ancient tomes defined.

Through whispers of the night wind's song,
Returns the force forgotten long.
Stars align in cosmic weave,
Crafting paths for spells to breathe.

In silent woods where old gods sleep,
Mystical power begins to seep.
Roots and leaves in unity,
Birth new realms of sorcery.

With dawn, the arcane force ignites,
Casting away the endless nights.
In rebirth, the power found,
Magic whispers the world around.

New Dawn of the Arcane

A whisper through the twilight's veil,
The ancient runes begin to sing,
A power surges, spirits sail,
To herald in an arcane spring.

Mystic lights the morning sky,
In hues of gold and violet hues,
Enchantment's breath, a gentle sigh,
As dawn unveils its secret muse.

The hidden realm, alive once more,
With echoes of a time long past,
Unlocks the knowledge, ancient lore,
As shadows flee, daylight vast.

Each leaf and stone, a magic thread,
Weaving tales of old rebirth,
As sunlight crowns the mystic bed,
A new dawn graces Mother Earth.

The arcane tides, they ebb and flow,
With every beat, the world aligned,
In every dawn, new forces grow,
To ever intertwine, entwined.

Lingering Echoes of Magic

In the quiet of the night,
When stars whisper secrets kept,
Magic's echoes take their flight,
In dreams where ancient power slept.

A gentle breeze, a silent call,
Echoes dance on moonbeam trails,
Memories rise, they never fall,
Through time's whispers, tales regale.

The shadows carry wistful tunes,
From epochs buried deep in mist,
Tracing patterns, old communes,
In the ether, spirits kissed.

Embers of the past ignite,
In the heart where echoes sing,
Lingering in the twilight,
A timeless dance on phantom wing.

Magic's presence, ever near,
In the world, subtle and true,
Whispers guide us, never fear,
In echoes' light, we're born anew.

Restoring Ethereal Grace

Beneath the canopy of stars,
Where ancient secrets softly weave,
A quest begins, no worldly bars,
For grace ethereal to retrieve.

In realms where shadows intertwine,
And moonlight dances on the lake,
The path is drawn in lines divine,
A heart's pure wish, a soul awake.

Through forests deep and mountains high,
Where eagles soar and rivers gleam,
Seek the grace that mystifies,
In every stone and silent dream.

Whispers draw from hidden springs,
A melody of olden time,
A song the wandering spirit sings,
In cadence pure, in rhythms chime.

The grace restored, a gentle peace,
Falls like dew on morning's face,
In unity, our spirits cease,
Restoring all with ethereal grace.

Making Magic Mine Again

In the quiet of my soul's retreat,
Where dreams and shadows intertwine,
I seek the magic, old yet sweet,
To claim it once again as mine.

Through mist and memory, I tread,
Along the paths once bathed in light,
Recalling words the ancients said,
Of spells that turned the dark to bright.

Hands outstretched to sky's embrace,
I feel the pulse of arcane streams,
In every breath, a whispered grace,
Echoes of my childhood dreams.

A spark ignites within my heart,
A flame that never truly died,
With each new dawn, a freshened start,
The magic flows, both deep and wide.

In every star and whispered breeze,
The secrets of the world align,
Embracing all with gentle ease,
I'm making magic mine again.

Finding My Inner Sorcery

In whispers of the twilight glow,
Where secret rivers softly flow,
I seek the power deep within,
To let the magic thus begin.

Beneath the stars, my heart does tread,
On paths that mystics often dread,
With every step, the veil does part,
Revealing sorcery of the heart.

Ancient runes and spells I find,
Etched in the corners of my mind,
A silent chant, a sacred spell,
Unlocking secrets none can tell.

In shadows cast by moonlit trees,
I dance upon the evening breeze,
Embracing all that lies in me,
The mystic force that sets me free.

No longer bound by doubts or fears,
I wield the power of my years,
Within my soul, the magic stirs,
A sorcerer's truth, the world confers.

The Revival of Wonder

Amidst the clang of daily life,
Where routine cuts like a knife,
I search for whispers of the old,
The wonders whispered tales unfold.

Through misty dawn and twilight's hush,
Where quiet dreams begin to rush,
I feel the wonder softly wake,
In every breath for magic's sake.

An ancient forest calls my name,
Its leaves, a-flutter, wild and tame,
Each step, a leap into the blend,
Of wonder's call, no longer penned.

Below the stars, in skies so clear,
The galaxies of wonder near,
With open heart and lifted eyes,
I see the world in pure surprise.

Revived, the wonder's spark does bloom,
A light that cuts the darkest gloom,
In every glance, in every sound,
The revival of wonder, profound.

Rediscovering Mystical Strength

In realms where shadows often creep,
Where dreams and fears together sleep,
I search for strength that's born of light,
To face the dark, to stand and fight.

The ancient mountains tell their tale,
Of warriors strong who never fail,
Their whispers guide me through the night,
To find within a mystic might.

In silent groves where spirits rest,
I feel the power within my chest,
A force of nature, clear and true,
Rediscovering strength anew.

With every breath, the courage grows,
In every leaf, the secret shows,
That deep within, we all possess,
A strength that's mystical, no less.

No chains can bind this inner fire,
No doubts can quell its fierce desire,
With newfound strength, I rise above,
Embracing all with mystic love.

Eclipsed No More

In shadows deep where secrets lie,
A hidden tear, a softened sigh,
I found a light that dared to gleam,
Eclipsed no more, it shared its dream.

Beneath the moon's enshrouded glow,
My heart began to feel and know,
That in the dark, a truth does burn,
A spark of hope, the tides do turn.

As dawn's first fingers touch the night,
The world awakes to endless light,
No longer hidden, strong and sure,
The soul within, eclipsed no more.

Through veils of doubt, I rise again,
To break the chains, to shed the pain,
For in my core, a luminesce,
A beacon bright, profound and dense.

With every step, the shadows flee,
With every breath, I claim to be,
A vessel filled with endless light,
Eclipsed no more, embracing might.

The Sorceress Unshackled

In shadows deep, where whispers sleep,
A sorceress found her name.
With chains unbound, on earthly ground,
She rose in untamed flame.

Her ears attuned to cosmic tears,
She danced with wild refrain.
A tempest born, her veil was torn,
No longer bound by pain.

A voice so clear dispelled her fear,
She called the spirits near.
Their secrets old, in tales untold,
Became her path to steer.

Midnight skies and moonlit eyes,
Her powers grew anew.
No longer slave, her heart was brave,
Her destiny she drew.

With magic free, her soul to see,
She banished dark despair.
The sorceress, in her caress,
Found light beyond compare.

The Mystical Awakening

Beneath the veil of twilight pale,
A stir within the air.
Magic awoke, the silence broke,
With whispers soft and rare.

The ancient rune beneath the moon,
Gave birth to light untamed.
A force so grand, by mortal hand,
Shall never be reclaimed.

As dawn unveiled, the spirits hailed,
A power long concealed.
With eyes aglow, the secrets flow,
In dreams, the truth revealed.

In forest deep where shadows creep,
A form began to rise.
With mystic art, it claimed a heart,
And sought to touch the skies.

Awakened mind, no longer blind,
Embraced the arcane lore.
With every breath, defying death,
It held the mystic core.

Reembracing the Arcane

Through ether's veil, where wild winds trail,
Old magics weave their charm.
A heart forlorn, now reborn,
Finds solace in the calm.

Whispers grand from spirit's hand,
Drew maps upon her soul.
In ancient signs and cryptic lines,
She saw the whole unfold.

The runes they sang, the echoes rang,
In corridors of time.
A symphony of memory,
In every whispered rhyme.

A lost spell's kiss, in twilight's mist,
Did softly call her name.
In arcane strive, she felt alive,
Her essence was the same.

Embracing lore, forever more,
She walked with eyes anew.
The arcane light, in darkest night,
Her spirit swiftly drew.

Reviving Celestial Magic

Beneath the stars, where ancient scars,
Hold tales of worlds unseen.
A magic bright, in moonlit night,
Revived a spectral sheen.

With cosmic keys, on astral seas,
The pathways clear and bright.
A sorcerer's art, in heaven's heart,
Unlocked the boundless light.

Spiral winds and comet spins,
Conspired to weave a spell.
Celestial lace in boundless space,
Where mystic secrets dwell.

The ethers sung where dreams are spun,
In harmonies of gold.
A reborn song, both pure and strong,
With power to behold.

In twilight's gleam, a timeless stream,
Revealed the magic's lore.
Celestial flame, reborn the same,
Ignites forever more.

Shadows of Forgotten Enchantments

In the twilight's gentle glow,
Whispers of old magic grow.
Hidden realms begin to stir,
Mysteries in shadows blur.

Ancient runes on weathered stone,
Secrets waiting to be known.
From the deep and darkened past,
Echoes of enchantments cast.

Moonlit dances on the breeze,
Weaving through the ancient trees.
Silent songs of times gone by,
Underneath a starlit sky.

Beneath the forest's emerald hue,
Lies the magic, pure and true.
Forgotten spells and hidden charms,
Cradle us in mystic arms.

Shadows lengthen, night grows deep,
In enchanted dreams, we sleep.
Guardians of lore and light,
Waking with the dawning night.

Reawakening Starborne Might

Beyond the realm of sight and sound,
Lost powers deep within are found.
Stars awaken, bright and bold,
Ancient tales once more are told.

Across the sky, a comet streaks,
A voice from long-lost epochs speaks.
Reviving strength within the core,
Heralding a power from before.

Galaxies in cosmic dance,
Weave a web of fate and chance.
Reawakening all that's right,
Borne within the starlit night.

Celestial bodies lend their flame,
To a world reborn in name.
With each spark of newborn light,
Rekindling the ancient might.

Witness now the rise anew,
Of powers that the heavens knew.
We, the vessels of their grace,
Stand in awe, our hearts embrace.

The Sorcery Within

Deep within the soul's dark well,
Lies a power none can quell.
Whispers of the arcane arts,
Stirring in our hidden hearts.

Binding words and secret rites,
In the dead of sleepless nights.
Sorcery within us lies,
Gaining strength beneath the skies.

Rituals of old and lore,
Open up the mystic door.
Drawing from the soul's deep core,
Powerful, yet seeking more.

In the quiet, midnight hour,
Feel the surge of hidden power.
Casting spells with every breath,
Binding fate and cheating death.

Mystic energies align,
Inner magic, soul divine.
Embrace the sorcery within,
Let the ancient dance begin.

Breathing Life into Spells

With a whisper and a sigh,
Magic drifts into the sky.
Air comes alive with the sound,
Mysteries weaving all around.

From the lips of sorcerers old,
Spells are cast, and tales are told.
Breathing life into the night,
With each word, the world ignites.

Candles flicker, shadows shift,
As incantations start to lift.
Murmured charms take to flight,
In the dark, a hidden light.

Spellbound winds begin to dance,
In an ancient, mystic trance.
Life and magic intertwined,
In the spell, our fate is signed.

Breathing life into the spell,
Waking powers dormant, fell.
Magic rises with each breath,
Overcoming time and death.

www.ingramcontent.com/pod-product-compliance
Lightning Source LLC
LaVergne TN
LVHW010554070526
838199LV00063BA/4964